Forensic

Putting the Pieces
Science Together

By M. Langley Biegert

Wright
Group

Forensic Science: Putting the Pieces Together
Copyright © 2005 Wright Group/McGraw-Hill
Text by Melissa Biegert

Explore More™ is a trademark of the McGraw-Hill Companies, Inc.

Wright Group/McGraw-Hill
P.O. Box 812960
Chicago, IL 60681
www.WrightGroup.com

Printed in Mexico

ISBN: 1-4045-2865-2
ISBN: 1-4045-2914-4 (6-pack)

5 6 7 8 9 10 RRM 10 09 08 07 06

Contents

Introduction

Shattered glass...missing diamonds...a partial footprint...strands of hair...

Does this sound like a case from a crime story or movie you have seen? Maybe so, but when real crimes are committed by real people, the investigators called to the scene must notice, collect, and test **evidence** so they can catch the criminal. They may use forensic science as they go into action.

So what is forensic science? The word *forensics* comes from a Latin word referring to public discussion. Today, **forensic science** refers to science used in legal cases, mostly criminal cases.

When law enforcement officials collect and test evidence, such as fingerprints, from a crime scene, they are using forensic science. When scientists testify in court about their examination of evidence, they are using forensic science. Many other professionals, such as doctors, dentists, geologists, computer programmers, artists, and even trained animals often use their expertise to help police carry out this important work. As advances in science have increased, so has the use of science in police work. Today, forensic science is considered a necessary part of law enforcement. Either side in a legal case may use forensic experts to support its arguments. Sometimes forensic scientists disagree about the results of tests because scientific testing is not always perfect. However, the use of forensic evidence does give greater objectivity to legal arguments by applying evidence to the laws of science. This sometimes helps to quickly settle legal cases if the forensic science clearly leads to one conclusion.

Expert forensic witnesses in a trial are supposed to be objective about the evidence, even if they might be getting paid by one side to testify in court. They are, above all, scientists.

Forensic science is also often used in legal cases that do not involve criminal activity. **Civil cases** may require forensic science and

lawyers to help prove their case. For example, someone may sue a neighbor because he believes the neighbor's dog damaged his property. In this case, a forensic expert might be called upon to test the evidence in order to connect the particular dog to the property damage.

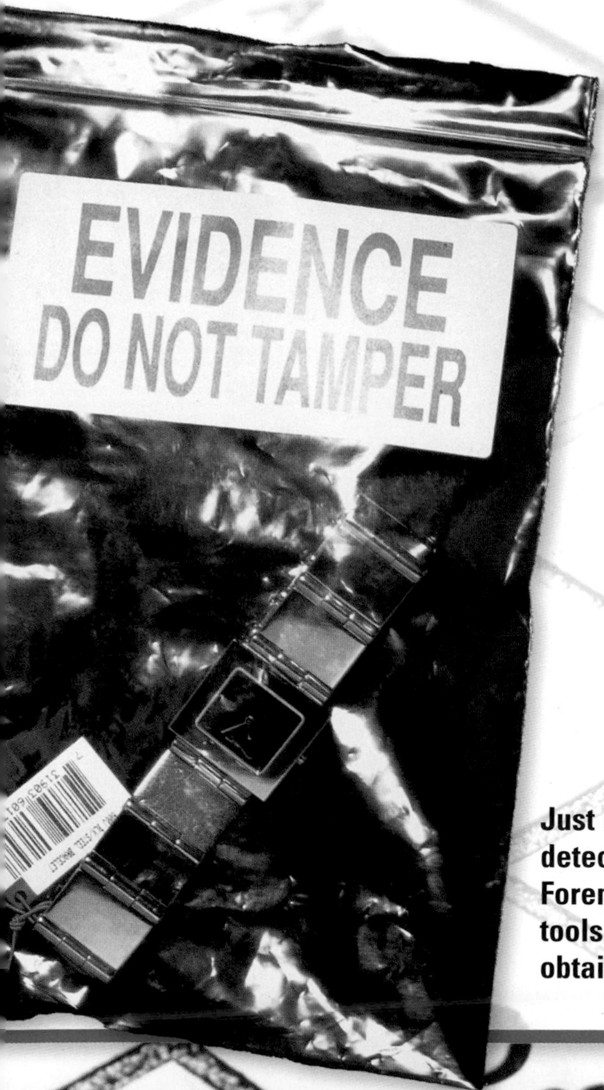

Today the use of forensic science is so common in the American legal system that it would be hard to imagine the system without it.

Just like a carpenter or plumber, a forensic detective also needs proper tools to do a good job. Forensic detectives must know how to use the tools correctly when they gather the evidence to obtain the most accurate information.

EVIDENCE
DO NOT TAMPER

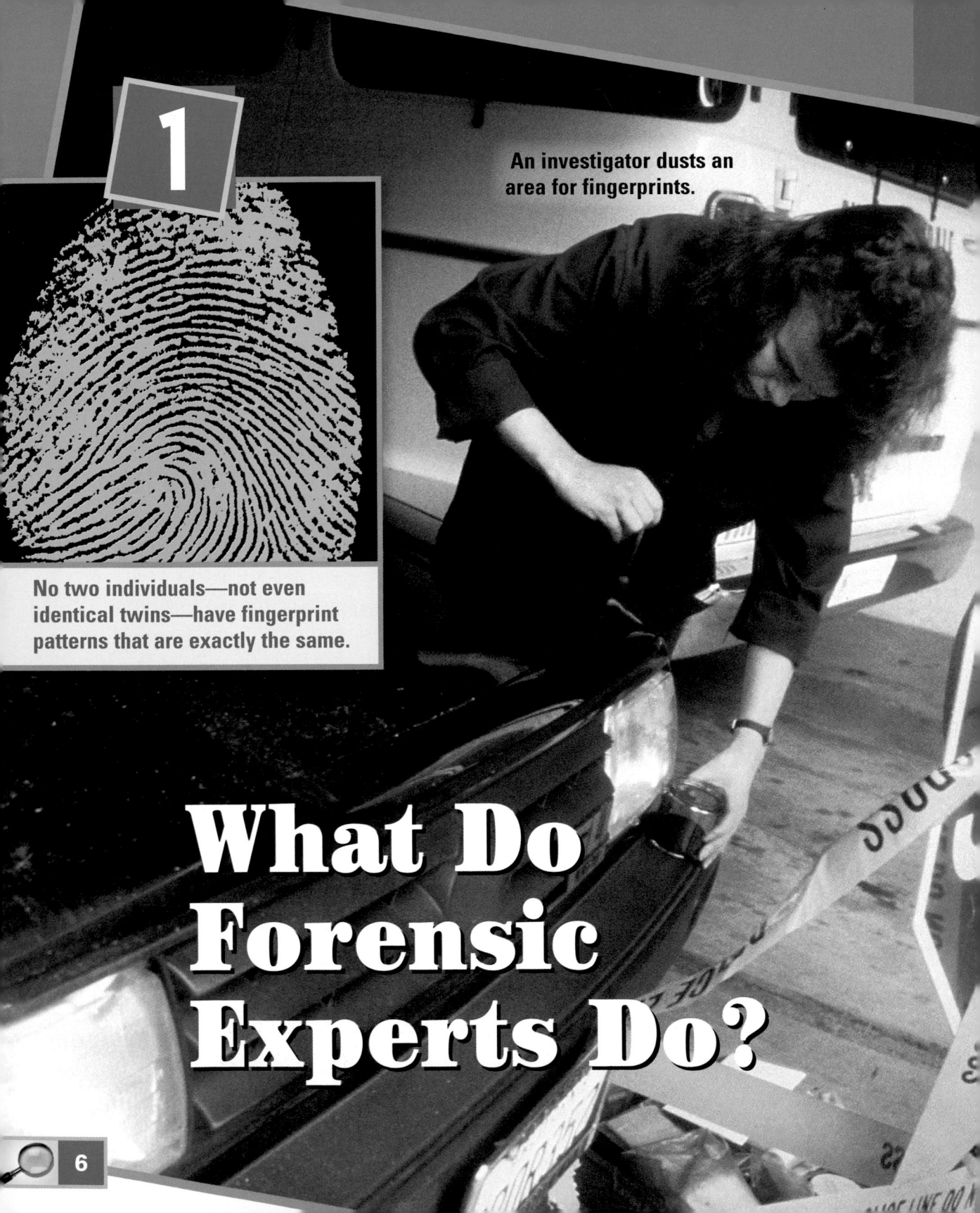

1

An investigator dusts an area for fingerprints.

No two individuals—not even identical twins—have fingerprint patterns that are exactly the same.

What Do Forensic Experts Do?

Forensic scientists study evidence—the material people present in court to "prove" their case. In court, evidence might be physical, such as a piece of recovered stolen merchandise, or it might be someone's testimony in court. Some of this testimonial evidence might involve eyewitness versions of what happened. Forensic scientists first examine the physical evidence, and then the scientists' official report or testimony in court often becomes evidence itself.

The earliest known forensic scientists were pathologists, medical doctors who study dead bodies to figure out the cause of death. This specialty has been practiced for centuries. In ancient China, officials called *death investigators* used forensic science and other methods to figure out how people died.

In 1248, a Chinese death investigator named Sung T'zu wrote the earliest known manual on forensic pathology. His book, *The Washing Away of Wrongs,* taught pathologists and other death investigators how to tell if someone's death resulted from murder or some other cause.

In one interesting case, Sung T'zu recalled how a village person appeared to have been murdered by a sickle, a common piece of farm equipment with a sharp, curved blade. A local death investigator asked all the village residents to bring their sickles to him for an examination. The death investigator noticed that one sickle attracted a lot of flies, which made him suspicious, since flies are often attracted to blood and tissue. Sure enough, upon closer examination of this sickle, the investigator found traces of the murder victim's blood and other tissue. The owner of the suspicious sickle quickly confessed to the murder. The importance of the flies in this case makes it one of the earliest examples of **forensic entomology.**

Fingerprint Patterns

Dactyloscopy, or using someone's fingerprints as a means of identification, helps law enforcement discover a suspect's true identity. Fingerprints are unique for each person. Law enforcement classifies fingerprints by the shapes of their raised ridges. A trained eye can recognize the four main classifications: loops, whorls, arches, and combinations of these. Loops often have U-shaped turns with a common center point. They

Loops

are the most common pattern and make up about seventy percent of all fingerprint patterns. Whorls show central ridges that turn through at least one complete circle. They are the next most common pattern at about twenty-five percent. Arches are recognized by their mound-like contour.

Whorls

Combination patterns show more than one feature.

Matching Evidence

From its early beginnings, the field of forensics continued to evolve and is still evolving today. In 1784, British police were trying to catch a killer who had used a pistol as a weapon. At that time pistols required "packing," small bits of wadded up paper placed inside the gun to help ignite the gunpowder that propelled the bullet. In this case, the killer had used a piece of torn newspaper to pack the gun. Police recovered the singed piece of newspaper from the gun and matched it to another torn piece of newspaper found in the suspect's pocket.

The matching of evidence to a specific person has always been very important to forensic work. In the late 1800s, for example, scientists realized that fingerprints are unique.

Did You Know?

People have a voiceprint, similar to a fingerprint. A sound spectrograph can measure the sound waves from a person's voice to produce a voiceprint that shows the pattern of these sound waves. Using this method, police can confirm the speaker of a recorded message.

Individual fingerprints can be identified by the patterns of shapes on them. Today, people who get arrested for a crime are always fingerprinted, and officials keep a record of those prints.

Latent Fingerprints

By the early 1900s, researchers figured out a way to pick up **latent fingerprints** left at a crime scene. Latent fingerprints cannot be seen by the naked eye. To make them visible, investigators "dust" a touched item with a dark powder that is made from chalk dust and other materials. They then "lift" the prints to make a permanent record of them. Tape or other adhesive material is placed over the visible prints, and then the tape is lifted. The image of the prints stays on the adhesive. Investigators may also take photographs of the visible prints. They can collect latent fingerprints at a crime scene and compare them with the suspect's fingerprints.

Fingerprints cannot be obtained from all materials. Rough surfaces like bricks, for example, usually will not produce a good latent print. Some law enforcement agencies, like the Federal Bureau of Investigation (FBI), have access to special equipment like

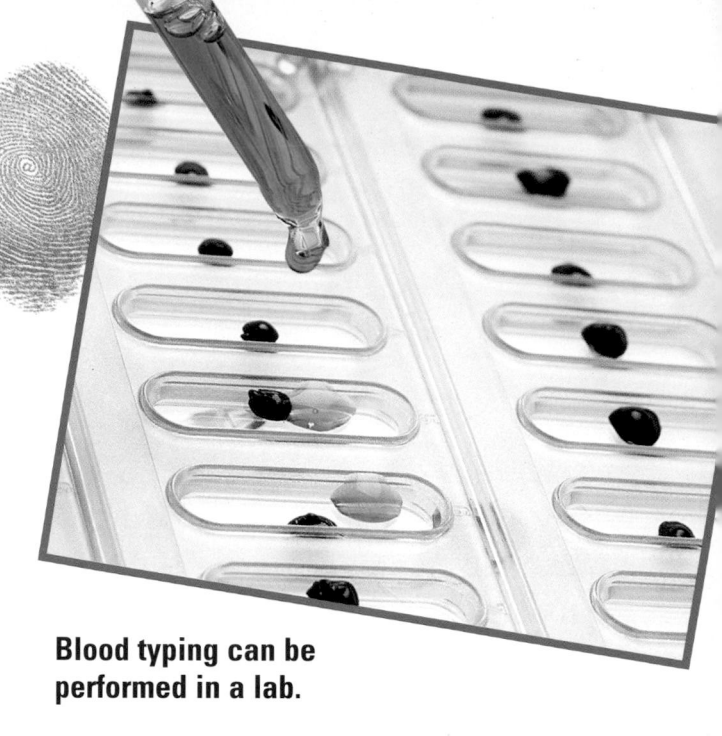

Blood typing can be performed in a lab.

lasers and powerful microscopes that can help them get hard-to-lift prints.

Blood and DNA Typing

The development of blood and DNA typing has also been helpful to the forensic study of physical evidence. In 1901, scientists discovered that human blood falls into four main types: A, B, AB, or O. Each blood type can also be either "positive," or "negative." Knowing this system can help rule out suspects in a crime. For example, if investigators know that the person who committed a crime has B-positive blood, then they can rule out any suspects with other types.

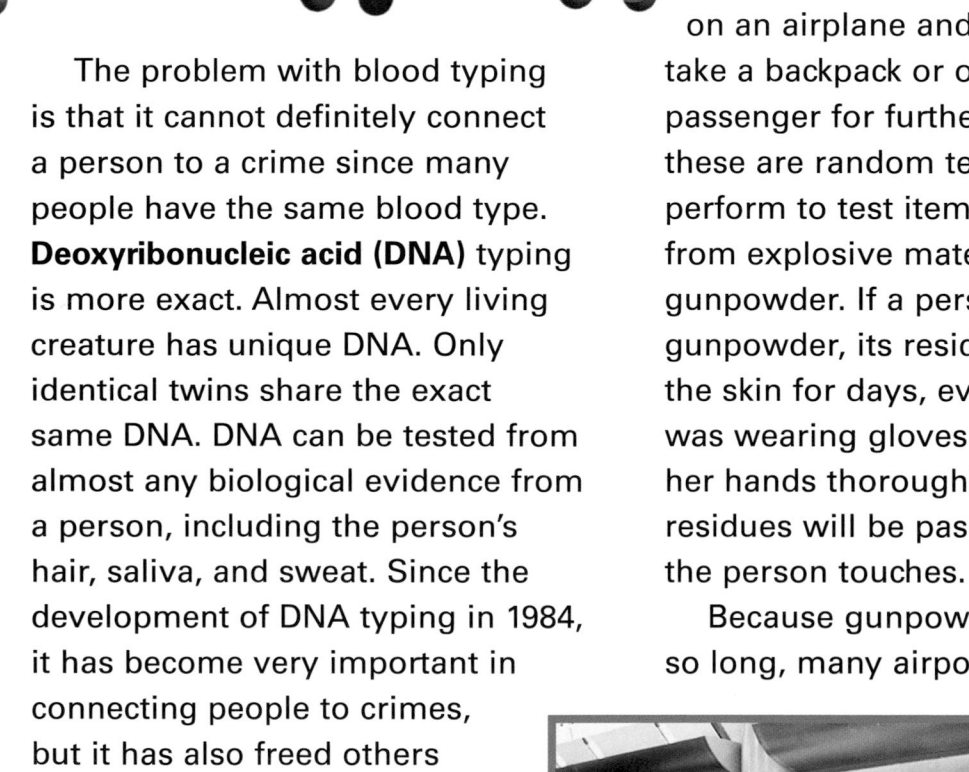

A molecular model of DNA looks like a double helix.

The problem with blood typing is that it cannot definitely connect a person to a crime since many people have the same blood type. **Deoxyribonucleic acid (DNA)** typing is more exact. Almost every living creature has unique DNA. Only identical twins share the exact same DNA. DNA can be tested from almost any biological evidence from a person, including the person's hair, saliva, and sweat. Since the development of DNA typing in 1984, it has become very important in connecting people to crimes, but it has also freed others mistakenly accused of crimes.

Trace Evidence

Rapid advances in scientific and technological knowledge in the twentieth century increased the impact of forensic science. For example, have you ever flown on an airplane and seen a screener take a backpack or other item from a passenger for further testing? Often these are random tests that screeners perform to test items for residues from explosive materials, such as gunpowder. If a person touches gunpowder, its residues will stay on the skin for days, even if the person was wearing gloves or washed his or her hands thoroughly. Traces of these residues will be passed onto anything the person touches.

Because gunpowder residues last so long, many airport passengers

Security at Honolulu Airport scans objects passing through an x-ray machine.

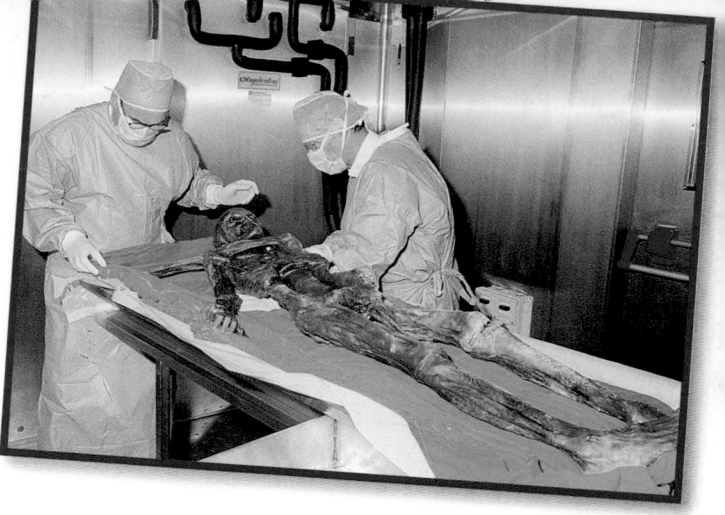

Scientists prepare "Otzi" in a museum in Italy.

may test positive for residues from harmless activities. For example, all fireworks contain gunpowder. If you shot off fireworks for the Fourth of July, and then flew on an airplane a few days later, you and your baggage would probably test positive for gunpowder residues. Luckily, just having gunpowder residues on you is not a crime, so you cannot be arrested for that alone. However, if a screening at an airport turns up gunpowder on you, the security officers will probably delay you for a long time while they make sure you and your baggage are safe to fly.

The main method of finding trace amounts of gunpowder from airport passengers is to use ion-mobility **spectrometers.** These are small microwave-type machines that test for explosive materials by heating up a sample of particles swabbed or vacuumed off the baggage. Another invention that can test for explosive residues on airport passengers is the Boarding Pass Analyzer. This device can test for any residues on boarding passes that passengers send through a small scanner.

Modern Forensic Science and the Iceman Mummy

Modern forensic science can even help solve ancient mysteries. In the summer of 2003, scientists performed new tests on the Iceman, nicknamed "Otzi," the world's oldest mummy. The 5,000-year-old mummy was discovered perfectly preserved in the frozen mountains of Italy in 1991. The cause of the Iceman's death has been a mystery. Although the mummy had an arrow wound to the back, new tests, including DNA testing performed on dried blood on his clothing, revealed the Iceman was probably killed in a fight with several other people. Because there are no other mummies to compare the other DNA to, there is no way of knowing exactly who killed the Iceman or why. The Iceman's death is now one of the world's oldest unsolved murder cases.

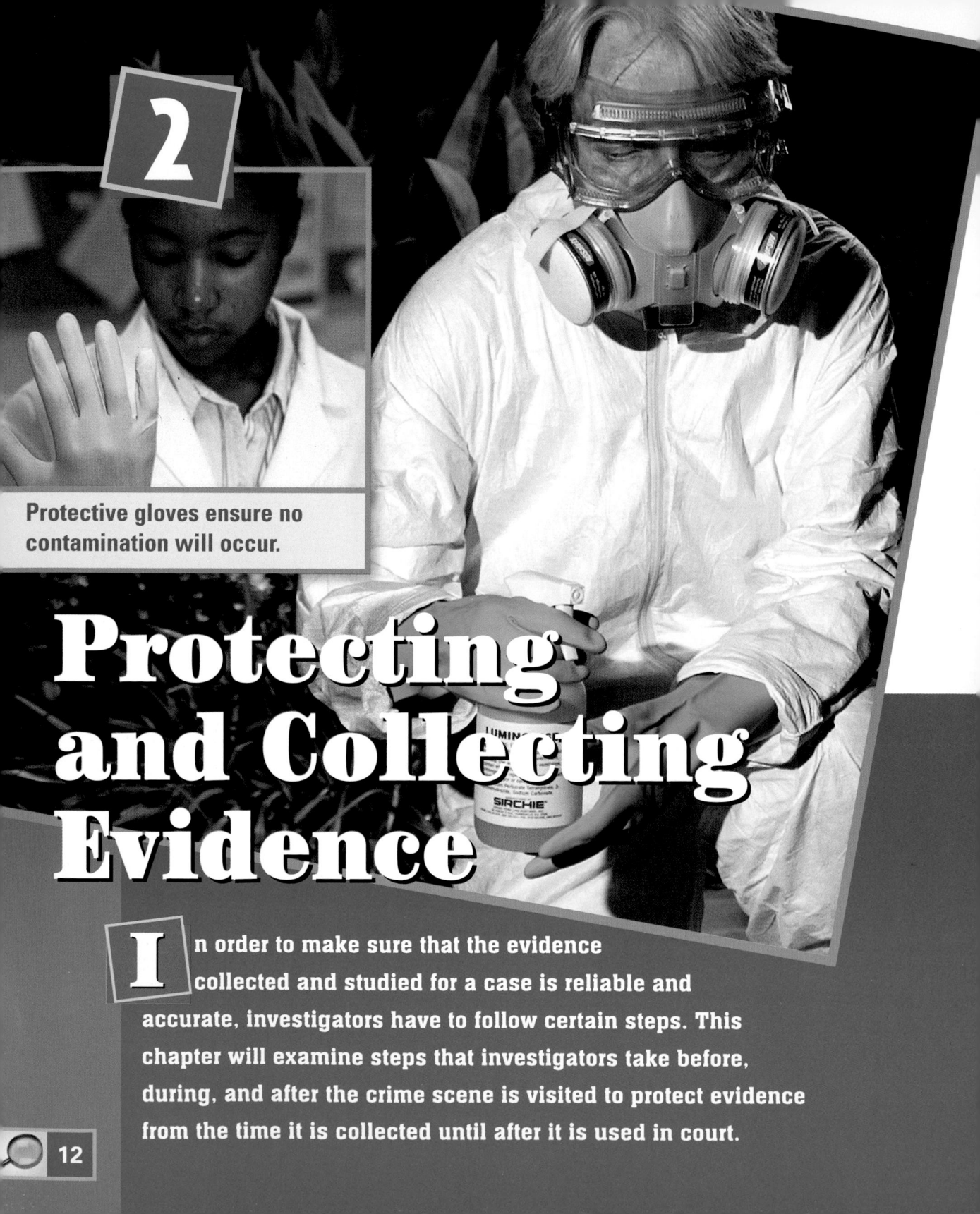

2

Protective gloves ensure no contamination will occur.

Protecting and Collecting Evidence

In order to make sure that the evidence collected and studied for a case is reliable and accurate, investigators have to follow certain steps. This chapter will examine steps that investigators take before, during, and after the crime scene is visited to protect evidence from the time it is collected until after it is used in court.

Protecting the Evidence and Investigators

Before a forensic investigator ever collects any evidence, he or she must make sure to use the proper protective equipment to safely gather it. Safety equipment includes barriers to stand between the investigator and the evidence, including gloves, protective eyewear, and other items. These items ensure that the evidence itself remains "clean" and free of contamination. If forensic evidence from a crime scene gets mixed in with materials from another source, test results could be altered. For example, if investigators picked up a piece of evidence with their bare hands, their fingerprints could smudge over existing fingerprints on the item. Investigators must also be sure that none of their DNA (such as blood from a cut) gets mixed up with the evidence so that the results of any DNA testing are not altered.

Using proper protective equipment also protects the health of the investigators. Evidence or a crime scene may contain materials that could harm someone who comes into contact with them. Protective equipment prevents investigators from coming into contact with bodily fluids, toxic substances like chemicals or poisons, or air at a crime scene that may be dangerous.

Investigators also follow careful procedures to protect the evidence once it is collected. They usually place it in a germ-free, protective container. Any bodily fluids are marked with a special sign and the word BIOHAZARD. Investigators are not allowed to eat, drink, or even apply makeup in the presence of potentially harmful materials. After gathering evidence, they sanitize their hands and the equipment they used.

Firefighters in protective suits remove a container of hazardous material.

Spotlight:
Analyzing a Crime Scene

While at the crime scene, investigators use collection and packaging materials, such as tamper-evident, sealed storage bags, for evidence. Their first focus is on evidence that could be lost or destroyed, such as a shoeprint. This evidence is collected first. Investigators gather all of the evidence and protect it from contamination by outside sources. They search the crime scene very carefully, beginning in accessible areas and moving outward toward the out-of-the-way places. Investigators must be sure that every trace of evidence is found. Sometimes this evidence can be hard to find, such as single hairs, small bits of dirt, or unseen fingerprints that can become the most important clues in solving a crime. Crime scene investigators also evaluate whether evidence appears to have been moved or manipulated into a scene that has been "set up."

Investigators interview witnesses to the event. If the witnesses can provide a good description, forensic artists will draw sketches of who or what they saw. These images are often used to help find suspects or other witnesses in the case.

Evidence from the suspect's clothing, such as footprints or even fibers, can be tested to find out exactly what type of clothing it was and possibly even what size it was. Since most people stand and walk in different ways, and thus leave a distinct "wear pattern" on their shoes, forensic experts can test these wear patterns to match a good footprint to the exact owner of the shoe.

DO NOT CROSS

Investigators collect any liquid evidence from the scene. If the liquid has dried, they must scrape up whatever they can to preserve for testing. Investigators prefer wet material to dry because the chemical or biological makeup of the liquid can change during the drying process.

Investigators examine any items that look out of place or which otherwise indicate they may be related to the crime. They may need to take measurements of items and reproduce sketches of the entire scene to use as evidence. Sometimes the placement or distance of items at a crime scene is just as important as the items themselves.

Investigators must dust any area that might contain fingerprints for unseen latent prints.

The crime scene photographer takes photographic images of the scene to preserve for future study or to use during a trial. It's much easier for a judge or jury to visualize what happened at a scene if they can actually see it in a photograph. Some crime scenes are also videotaped. Sometimes investigators can look at a photograph from a crime scene and spot something they might have missed seeing when they were actually there.

Investigators collect small hairs that can be used to identify people who have been at the scene. Hair analysis used to rely mainly on matching patterns in hair strands under a microscope. Now individual hairs can be used in DNA testing for more reliable matching.

DO NOT CROSS

One of the first things investigators do to protect the evidence is to seal off the crime scene area, usually with crime scene tape like this. The area will usually remain sealed off until the investigation is complete.

Maintaining the Chain of Custody

All information and evidence associated with a crime must be carefully collected, labeled, organized, and stored. If an investigator writes notes in a notebook at a crime scene, these notes also become protected evidence.

Once the evidence is collected at the crime scene, investigators must make sure that it is stored properly and only handled by trained people.

The process of handling the evidence after it is collected is called the **Chain of Custody**. In most cases, once the evidence is collected, a log is kept of everyone who handles the materials. If the evidence is damaged or disappears, the chain of custody log can determine who last handled the materials. Although rules regarding the handling of evidence vary, the flowchart below illustrates the typical Chain of Custody process for handling evidence.

THE CHAIN OF CUSTODY

At every stage in the Chain of Custody, the handlers of the material must sign the Chain of Custody record to keep track of who has the evidence.

Investigators collect forensic evidence at the crime scene.

The investigators carefully place the evidence in a germ-free, protective container.

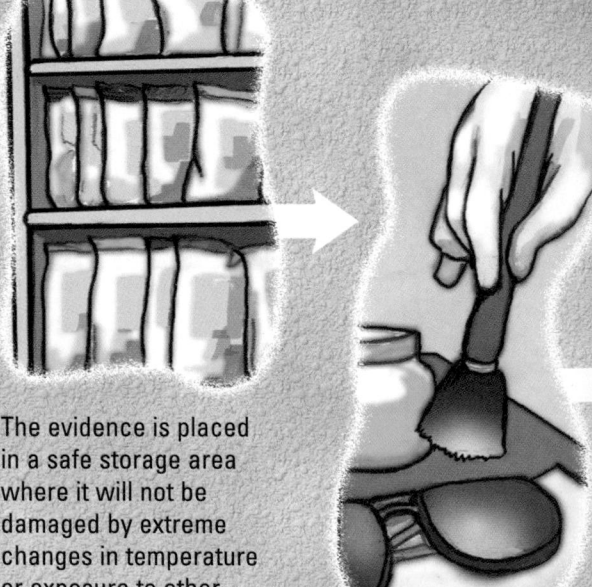

The evidence is placed in a safe storage area where it will not be damaged by extreme changes in temperature or exposure to other materials.

Forensic scientists conduct the appropriate tests on the materials.

Crime scene photographers take images of all the important evidence at a scene.

After all tests have been completed, the evidence is returned to a safe storage area.

The evidence is presented during trial for the legal case.

After the legal case is completely finished, the evidence may either continue to be stored, it may be properly destroyed, or it may be returned to the original owner of the material. Rules for the final disposal of evidence vary and depend largely on the type of evidence and whether there may be an appeal of the original court case.

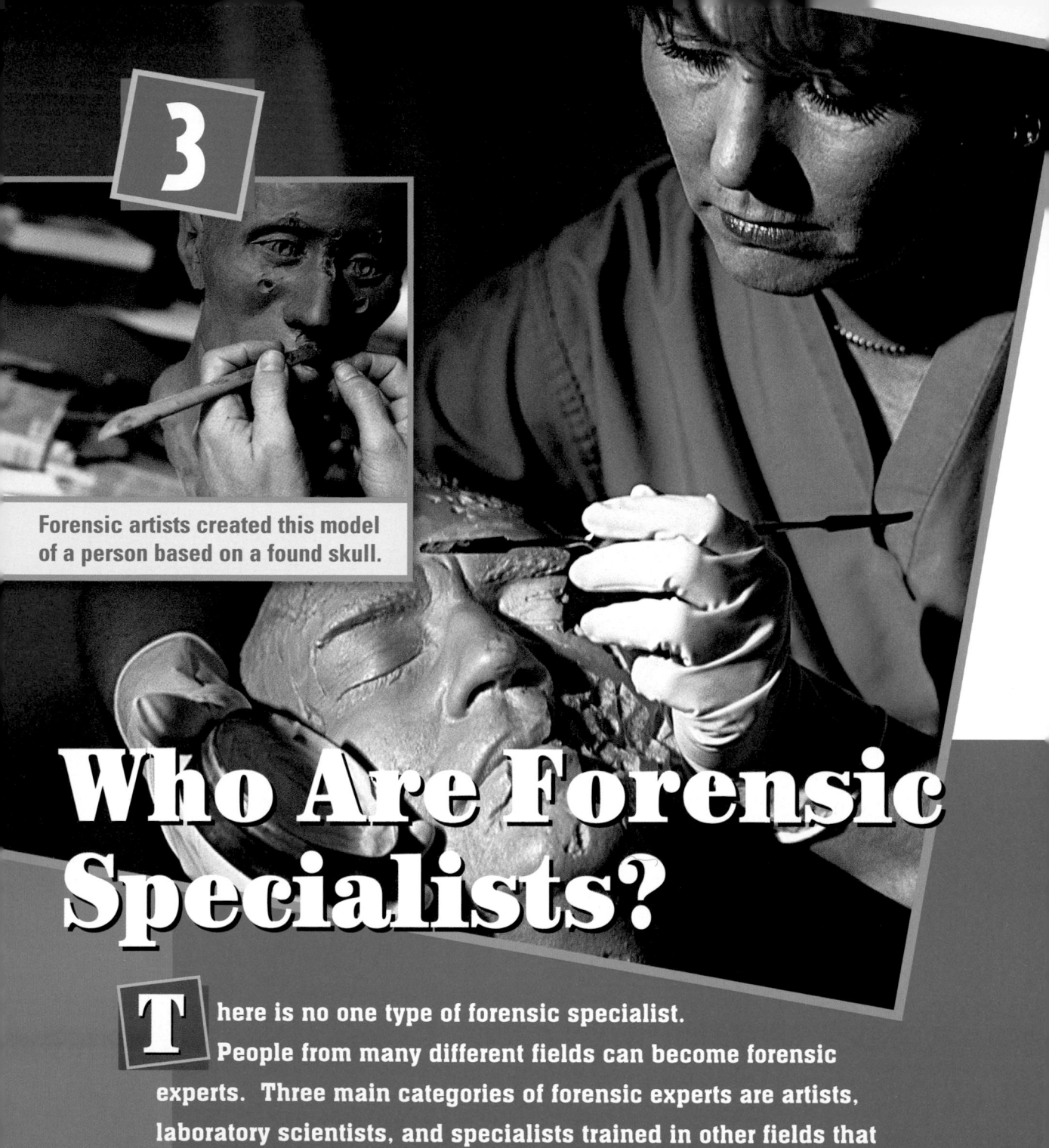

3

Forensic artists created this model of a person based on a found skull.

Who Are Forensic Specialists?

T here is no one type of forensic specialist. People from many different fields can become forensic experts. Three main categories of forensic experts are artists, laboratory scientists, and specialists trained in other fields that lend their assistance to analyze unusual forensic evidence. But first, how do you become a forensic expert?

Forensic science is so common that some colleges now offer degrees. Because forensic specialties vary, they require different types of courses and training. Most specialties require a strong background in math and sciences, such as chemistry and biology, along with skills in writing and communication.

The Artists

Forensic art can help find a missing person or crime victim or identify the remains of a dead person. In the case of a criminal suspect, forensic artists will usually interview witnesses or victims of the crime and develop a composite sketch of the suspect. This process requires more than just artistic skill. People's memories of events, especially traumatic ones, can differ greatly, and sometimes people can recall new details long after the events have passed. The forensic artist must listen carefully to all of the descriptions to put together the most likely image of what the suspect looks like.

Becoming a forensic artist requires extensive artistic training, especially in human anatomy. Forensic artists must understand how the movable frame of the skeleton works together with each body system and each muscle. Forensic artists also need to know how the human body changes over time. They may need to create an image of what a person looked like before death, and they must take into consideration how death can change a person's appearance.

Sometimes forensic artists need to create a sculpture of a face based only on a skeleton. They recreate the face based on what they understand about the way muscles and skin lay over the human skull. Forensic artists often work closely with **forensic anthropologists** to recreate a face based only on a skeleton.

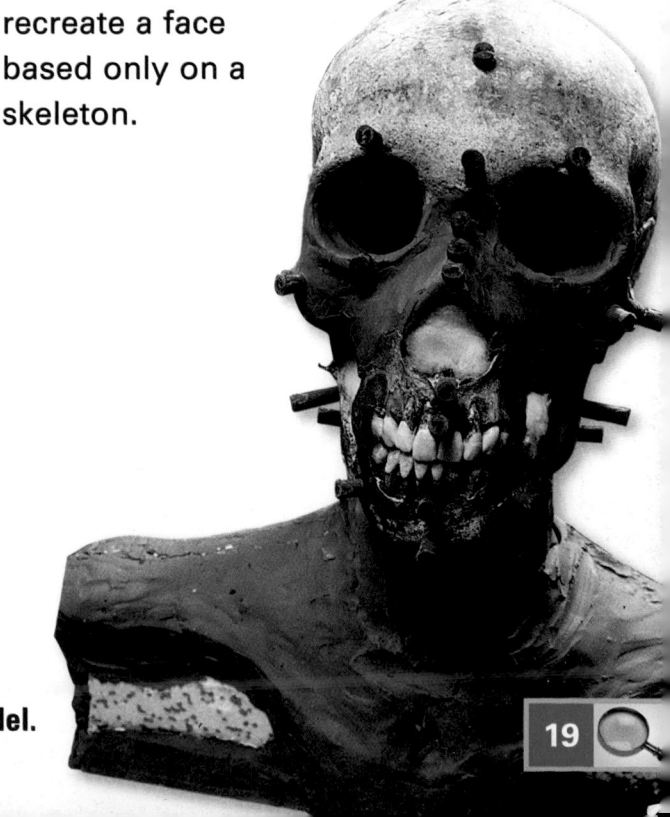

This skull was pieced together on a clay model.

accurate portrait.

Laboratory Scientists

Laboratory scientists conduct different types of tests on forensic evidence. Forensic laboratory researchers include pathologists, **toxicologists, serologists,** chemists, and **ballistics** experts.

Pathologists sometimes work closely with toxicologists to figure out what caused a person's death. When someone dies under suspicious circumstances or for unknown reasons, a toxicologist will perform tests on the person's blood to determine if drugs, alcohol, or some other substance played a role in the death. Forensic serologists are the people who perform laboratory tests on bodily fluids, such as blood or saliva.

Forensic chemists test substances that are not from or within a human body. For example, they can test suspected drug evidence to determine if it is an illegal substance. They can match chemicals such as dyes from the scene of a crime with chemicals found on a suspect's clothing.

One of the trickiest tasks for forensic artists is to develop an image of a person who has been missing for many years, such as a child. In such cases, the artist must take the last known photograph of the person and "age" it to show what the person probably looks like now. To "age" a face, forensic artists need to know how the bones of the face grow. Computer programs can help the artists create an aged image, but it still takes a great deal of skill to produce an

Ballistics experts learn a lot from recovered bullets, such as these .38s.

They can even match the type of ink used in a note to the bottle of ink it came from. Chemists also test many unknown substances to determine exactly what they are.

Forensic science in the laboratory has been greatly aided by improvements in the microscope over the past 100 years. Microscopes help researchers see tiny bits of evidence hidden to the naked eye.

How do forensic experts know if a bullet used in a crime came from the suspect's gun? Ballistics experts can match a bullet to the gun used to shoot it by examining the patterns left by the bullet. Sometimes the ballistics expert only has part of a bullet recovered at a crime scene. Because different guns use bullets of different sizes and strengths, the forensic expert can check the size, shape, and even the covering of the bullet to determine what kind of gun it came from.

Once a gun that is suspected of

being used in the crime has been obtained, the ballistics expert can perform more tests to match the weapon to the spent bullet fragment. These tests usually involve shooting the gun again several times in a safe environment and matching the markings on the spent bullets to the ones recovered at the crime scene. Every gun leaves unique, tiny markings on a bullet it discharges.

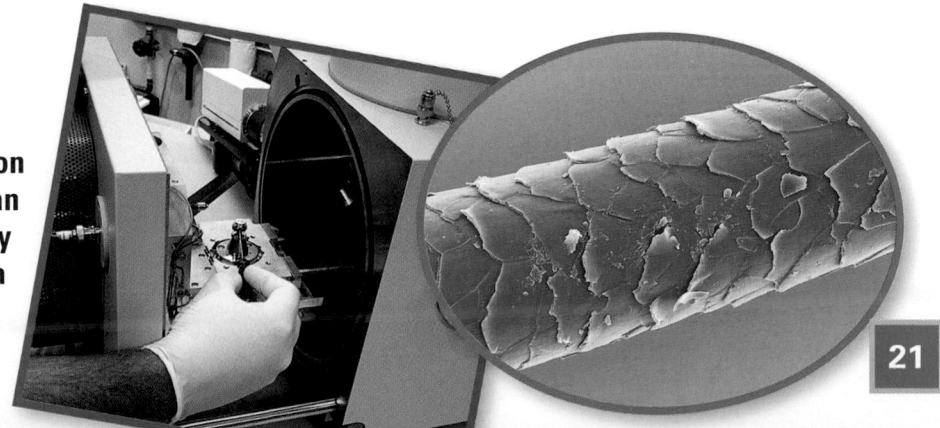

Scanning electron microscopes can examine tiny surfaces, such as a human hair (right).

Other Specialists

Some forensic experts are specialists in certain fields unrelated to law enforcement. They are called upon from time to time to lend their expertise in unusual criminal or civil cases that might go to court. Some of these specialists include entomologists, anthropologists, and dentists.

A common expert witness in trials is a **psychologist** or **psychiatrist.** These experts study the human mind and behavior. Psychologists usually have a doctoral degree, while psychiatrists are medical doctors who specialize in psychology. They often interview witnesses or suspects in a case in order to answer questions about that person's mental state. Such testimony can influence what a jury or judge believes about the statements of the person in question.

Another type of expert who often testifies in court cases is a document examiner. A document examiner specializes in spotting forged documents and often works for private companies, such as banks or government agencies,

that are concerned about getting fake documents. Their special training allows them to spot small abnormalities in documents, such as minor differences in handwriting, that indicate if the signature is real. It takes a fine eye for detail to become a document examiner.

Another rapidly growing field is **computer forensics.** As computers have become mainstream, they have also become important sources of evidence. Computers believed to contain evidence for cases can be seized and all of the files stored on them examined.

A DNA expert for the FBI holds up a sealed evidence bag during his testimony.

Even when you erase a file from your computer, it leaves an impression "ghosted" somewhere in the computer. A good computer expert can find ways of uncovering this erased material and retrieving it for use as evidence.

The expansion of the Internet increased online crimes. Some people try to illegally "hack" into other computer systems to cause harm. Computer forensic experts are responsible for tracking down the source of such illegal activity. For example, in the late 1990s an international gang of hackers called the Phonemasters illegally gained access to numerous companies (including major telephone companies), parts of a grid that controls most of the country's electrical power, and air traffic control centers. Investigators caught the suspects by analyzing information from the phone lines connected to the attacked groups. Through this process they were able to backtrack and capture the suspects' communications data.

An expert in almost any field may be called upon to analyze forensic evidence. For example, geologists have been called upon to identify rocks and dirt found in connection with a case. An expert automobile mechanic might be called to testify about damage done to a car. An engineer might be called upon to testify about the structural integrity of a building. If you ever become an expert at something, you never know when your skills might be called upon in a court of law.

This fictional case involves stolen diamonds!

Forensics in Action: Solving a Case

Now that you know how forensic science is used in criminal cases, let's see what it feels like to be a detective. In this chapter, you can use what you've learned to help solve a case. As you read through the description of the crime, think about what information would be useful to a forensic scientist and what tests he or she might use to solve the case.

The Crime

It is 2 A.M. on Thursday morning, and there has been a break-in at Crowell's Jewelry Store on the corner of Main Street and Vine Boulevard. The streetlight at the corner is burned out so the street is very dark. Thieves have cut a hole in the glass front door of the store, reached in, and turned the lock.

A little blood is on the door. The thieves have disabled the burglar alarm. Before the thieves disabled the video camera, it recorded the masked intruders entering the store. Explosives were used to blow open the safe. A large number of loose diamonds are missing. Smudges of burned powder are on the floor surrounding the safe, and there is a partial shoeprint in the powder.

Down the street from the jewelry store is the All-Night Convenience Store. One customer and a clerk at the store heard a loud noise coming from the jewelry store at about the same time the burglary took place. As the customer was leaving the All-Night Convenience Store, he witnessed two people running away from Crowell's Jewelry Store. The customer shouted at them, but they ran faster toward a dark blue car on the next corner. A piece of paper with some numbers written on it dropped out of the pocket of one of the people as they ran. The blue car, which had a very dirty license plate, quickly sped away.

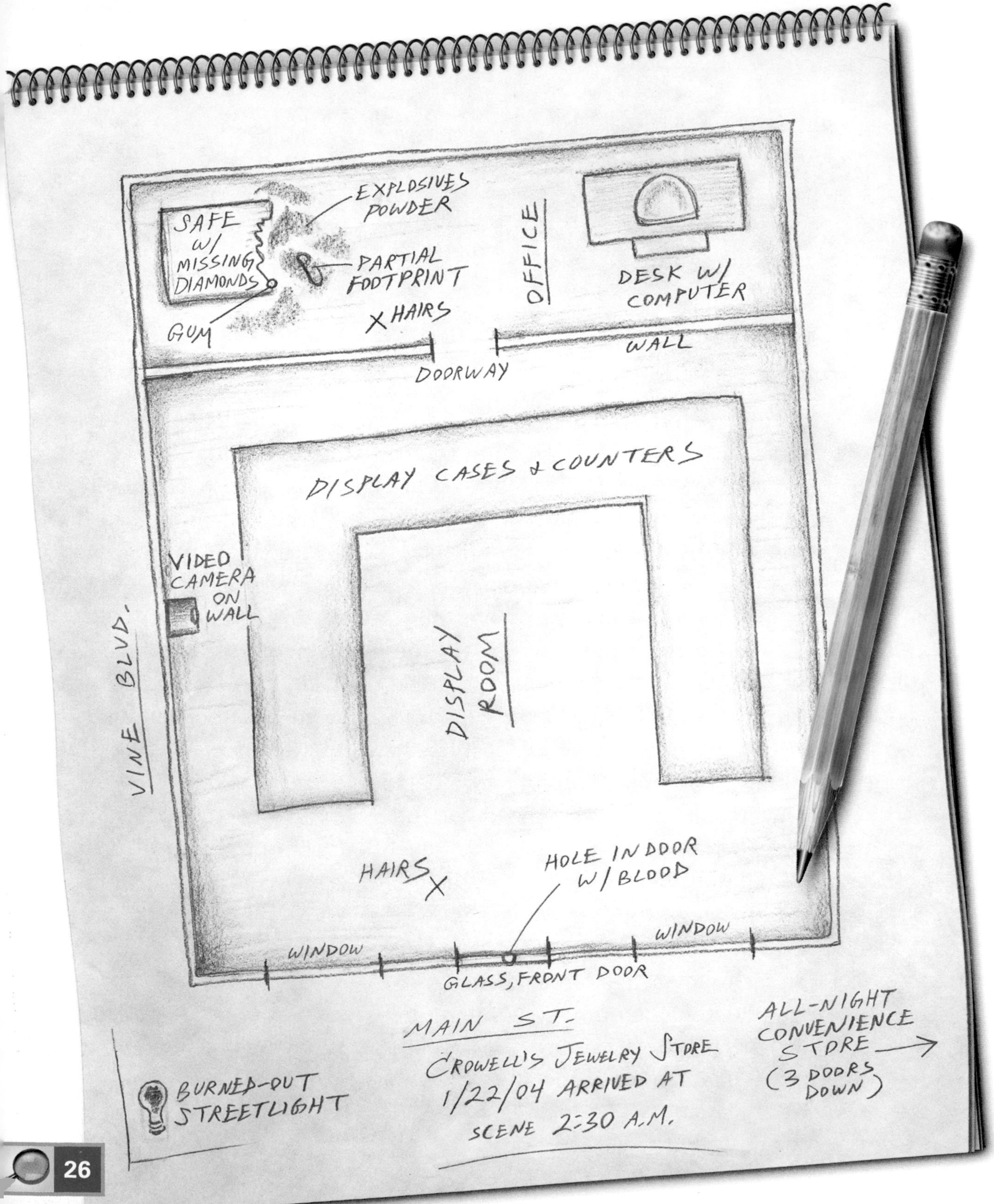

SAFE W/ MISSING DIAMONDS

EXPLOSIVES POWDER

PARTIAL FOOTPRINT

X HAIRS

GUM

OFFICE

DESK W/ COMPUTER

WALL

DOORWAY

DISPLAY CASES & COUNTERS

VIDEO CAMERA ON WALL

DISPLAY ROOM

VINE BLVD.

HAIRS X

HOLE IN DOOR W/ BLOOD

WINDOW

WINDOW

GLASS, FRONT DOOR

MAIN ST.
CROWELL'S JEWELRY STORE
1/22/04 ARRIVED AT
SCENE 2:30 A.M.

ALL-NIGHT CONVENIENCE STORE →
(3 DOORS DOWN)

BURNED-OUT STREETLIGHT

The Crime Scene

When police arrive at the scene and begin to gather evidence, they find two sets of hairs. They also find a chewed-up piece of gum, which appears to have been used as an adhesive to help stick the explosive materials onto the safe.

The Solution

When you and your team arrive on the scene, you are immediately aware of some very important clues. The blood on the door will yield DNA evidence. The tool used to cut the glass might have left a very unique pattern, much like a fingerprint. These thieves were very careless. The shoeprint one of them left in the explosive powder and the residue that is probably still on the suspects will make it easier to connect them to the crime scene once they are found. Your team of experts goes to work securing the area and collecting the evidence. The forensic artist interviews the witness from the All-Night Convenience Store and puts together a sketch. Even though the burglars were masked, the witness suggests that they are both men and easily describes their clothing. The video image matches the eyewitness description. The witness also gives an estimate of the suspects' height and weight. The witness had a partial view of the driver in the blue car, a woman. The forensic artist puts together a sketch of the driver based on the eyewitness account. The car is a four-door sedan, but the witness cannot recall the numbers because of the dirty license plate.

A forensic serologist analyzes the blood found on the door of the jewelry store and says that it belongs to someone with A-positive blood. Investigators speculate that one of the thieves was cut by broken glass while trying to open the door by reaching his hand through the hole that was cut. The DNA of the blood on the door is tested and matched to the DNA from one of the hair samples found at the scene. DNA tests performed on the chewing gum match the DNA of the other hair sample.

In some small communities, one person may have to serve as pathologist, toxicologist, and serologist. Many states have forensic laboratories that can serve smaller communities, and the FBI laboratory will assist in some cases.

The numbers on the dropped piece of paper are the code to the jewelry store's alarm. Tests performed on the note with the security code show that the note was written in black ink on a notepad made by Office King products. Upon questioning, the owner of Crowell Jewelry Store says he kept a copy of the security code in a file on his office computer. Computer forensics experts perform tests on the owner's computer and determine that someone has recently hacked into it, probably to gain access to the security code. The computer experts trace the hacking back to a computer owned by a Ms. Terry Carter. A check of vehicle records shows that Ms. Carter owns a dark blue four-door sedan.

Police question Ms. Carter, a computer programmer, who also happens to match the forensic artist's sketch of the getaway driver. The police obtain a search warrant to gather evidence at Ms. Carter's home. Her home computer is tested and confirmed to be the one that hacked into the jewelry store's computer. A notepad made by Office King is confiscated from her home as well. Impressions tests reveal the image of the code numbers pressed into the notepad as a result of someone writing a previous note containing the numbers on top of it. Police also find traces of nitroglycerin, incriminating evidence since dynamite was used to blow the safe open, as well as hairs that match the ones found at the scene of the crime.

Despite all the evidence, Ms. Carter refuses to cooperate with the police. Upon questioning Ms. Carter's neighbors, police learn that Ms. Carter's brother works in

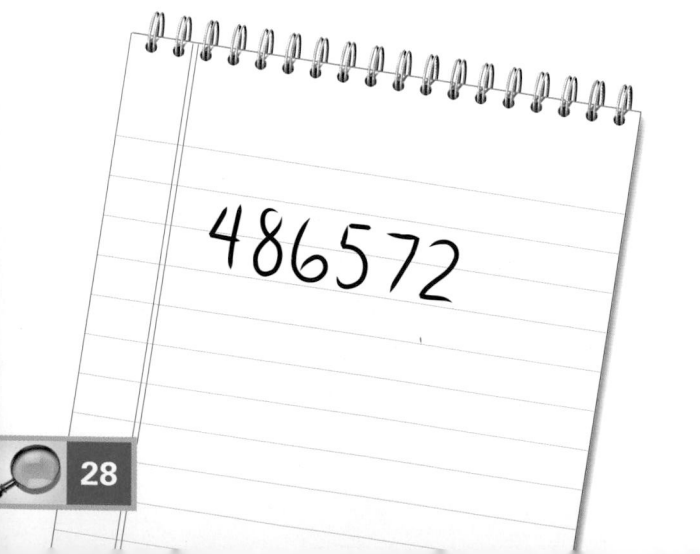

Collecting Fingerprints

In 1924, the FBI started a collection of fingerprints already taken from people. By the early 21st century, the FBI collection had grown to over 250 million fingerprints. The FBI has been moving this collection to a computer database so that by the touch of a keystroke they can match a latent print to the owner if his or her prints are on file. This process is especially helpful in catching career criminals who continue to commit crimes after getting out of prison.

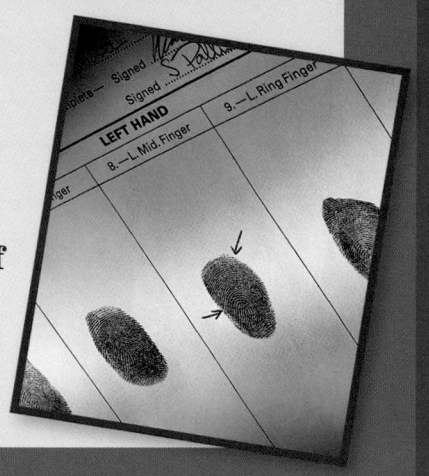

a demolition business that recently reported some stolen dynamite.

The brother's boss turns over a sample of a report the brother filled out at work to the police. A document examiner determines that the brother's handwriting on the work report matches the handwriting on the note dropped at the jewelry store. The work report also contains traces of the brother's DNA, which is tested and matched to the DNA on the gum and hair evidence collected at the jewelry store. However, a search of the brother's home turns up no diamonds.

So what happened to the diamonds? And who owns the other DNA sample? Ms. Carter and her brother are still not talking. So police run the DNA sample through a database containing thousands of DNA samples taken from previously arrested people. The database matches the DNA sample to Phillip Johnson, a career burglar recently released from jail. The diamonds are found in Johnson's home.

As it turns out, the Carters agreed to help Johnson rob the jewelry store. It took all three of them to do the job—Johnson's skills as a burglar, Ms. Carter's knowledge of computers, and her brother's access to dynamite and knowledge of explosives. In the end, though, their crime was foiled by the work of investigators and modern forensic science.

A specialist can interpret DNA fingerprinting as shown here.

Conclusion

Just like the missing piece in a puzzle, forensic science helps investigators link criminals to crimes. The case you have just read is not real, but the forensic science described could be. Every day, law enforcement officials use the skills of forensic science to solve cases and carry out justice. Using science as evidence provides an objective way to get at the truth of what happened in certain situations.

However, the scientific facts alone won't get the job done! Forensic science depends on many different experts with many different skills. They are highly trained professionals who sometimes deal with technical equipment and exacting forensics testing procedures.

Modern forensic science gives law enforcement officials a powerful tool for catching criminals and solving crimes. What will you think about the next time you watch a crime story on television? Will you be able to identify forensic-science methods? Imagine the new forensic-science technologies that will be possible in the future. Who knows? Maybe one day you will be a forensic expert, providing the missing link to an "unsolvable" case. Case closed!

Forensic scientists piece clues together to solve a case.

Glossary

ballistics study of the movement and impact of items propelled through the air

Chain of Custody process of handling evidence after it is collected

civil cases legal cases that do not involve criminal activity

computer forensics scientific examination and analysis of data retrieved from computer storage

deoxyribonucleic acid (DNA) chemical that contains the gene pattern that makes up a living creature

evidence material people present in court to "prove" their case

forensic anthropologists experts who apply skeletal and biological principles to identify skeletal and human remains

forensic art type of art that helps authorities identify, catch, or convict a criminal

forensic entomology field that uses scientific knowledge of bugs and their behavior to examine evidence

forensic science science used in legal cases, mostly criminal cases

latent fingerprints fingerprints left by the oils on a person's hand whenever he or she touches something

psychiatrist a medical expert who studies the human mind and behavior

psychologist an academic expert who studies the human mind and behavior

serologists scientists who perform laboratory tests on bodily fluids

spectrometers small microwave-type machines that test for explosive materials

toxicologists scientists who examine the harmful effects of chemicals or drugs on living creatures

Index